THE RAT

For Luna

Library and Archives Canada Cataloguing in Publication

Gravel, Elise
[Rat. English]
        The rat / Elise Gravel.

(Disgusting critters)
Translation of: Le rat.
ISBN 978-1-77049-659-0 (paperback)

        I. Rats--Juvenile literature. I. Title. II. Title: Rat. English.
III. Series: Gravel, Élise. Disgusting critters.

QL737.R666G7213 2016   j599.35'2   C2015-906948-3

Published simultaneously in the United States of America by Tundra Books of Northern New York,
a division of Random House of Canada Limited, a Penguin Random House Company

Library of Congress Control Number: 2013953639

English edition edited by Samantha Swenson
Designed by Elise Gravel and Tundra Books
The artwork in this book was rendered digitally
Printed and bound in China

www.penguinrandomhouse.ca

1 2 3 4 5 6   21 20 19 18 17 16

Elise Gravel

THE RAT

HI!

Tundra Books

Ladies and gentlemen, let me introduce you to your new disgusting little friend:

THE RAT.

The most common rats are
the brown rat and the black rat.
In Latin, the black rat is called

RATTUS
RATTUS.

The rat looks a bit like a

MOUSE.

She has a long tail, sharp teeth and a pointy nose. But she is usually much bigger (and meaner!) than a mouse.

The rat's tail is long, hairless and very agile. She uses it to keep her balance, and she sometimes wraps it around objects to lift them or hang on to them— it's almost like having a

FIFTH PAW.

It's also very useful when I want to pick my nose.

The rat is a real

ATHLETE.

She can swim, jump high and far, run fast and squeeze her body through holes as small as a quarter.

25¢

The rat has four long, yellowish

iNCiSORS

(big teeth) that are very sharp. They can grow up to 5 inches (13 centimeters) a year. To keep them from growing too long, the rat has to file them by

CHEWING ON STUFF.

Her teeth are very

TOUGH!

She can chew on practically anything: electrical wires, cement, wood, plastic, cardboard—you name it!

The rat likes to live near humans so that she can help herself to our food and our

GARBAGE.

I'd like some more of those delicious electrical wires in tomato sauce.

The rat is

VERY RUDE.

She doesn't mind doing her business
wherever she feels like it, and that
includes our pantries. She can transmit
a lot of

DISEASES,

some of them nasty.

She is also very

INTELLIGENT.

She's capable of learning lots of things, finding her way through difficult mazes and solving complicated

PROBLEMS.

By observing rats,

SCIENTISTS

learn important things that they can use to help humans.

Interesting!

The rat is a good laboratory animal because, like us, she's a

CLEVER

mammal, and also because some of her

BEHAVIORS

resemble ours.

Even though most people find rats disgusting, some find them

REALLY CUTE

and keep them as pets.

So next time you meet a rat, be nice.
You never know, maybe one day she'll
help you do your

HOMEWORK!